GARLIC

THE GOODNESS OF
GARLIC

40 AMAZING IMMUNE-BOOSTING RECIPES

NATASHA EDWARDS
PHOTOGRAPHY BY PETER CASSIDY

KYLE BOOKS

CONTENTS

GARLIC IS GREAT

How can something so healthy also taste so good? It's a shame we can't say this about all the delicious things in life but happily with garlic, we can as it has both – health benefits and flavour – in abundance. I grew up with garlic – on Mersley Farm, now popularly known as 'the garlic farm' on the Isle of Wight – and so inevitably it has played a very big role in my life. And yet, incredibly, years and years of planting, harvesting, cleaning, plaiting, cooking, tasting and talking about garlic have done nothing to dampen my enthusiasm for the affectionately named 'stinking rose'. I love garlic and all my family are what you might call devoted 'alliophiles'. The plant has a natural magnetism: it draws people in, amuses, excites and inspires and as you are reading this book, it's likely that garlic has already lured you in some way too. Perhaps you already add the odd clove to your cooking or maybe you are intrigued by stories of garlic's therapeutic properties. Whatever your existing relationship with garlic, my mission is to encourage you to use more of it – for its wonderful flavour and its many health benefits too.

PREPARING

The most exciting thing about garlic is how much its flavour varies according to the way it is prepared. Chopping or crushing a clove yields that distinctive pungent aroma and tastes strongest.

This is because damaging the clove triggers a powerful chemical reaction that produces allicin, which is largely responsible for garlic's heat and strong smell. For this reason, garlic tastes milder and sweeter when cooked whole.

quality garlic crusher will leave less waste and be easier to clean.

Bashing the garlic in a pestle and mortar will achieve a similar flavour but different consistency. If you cook crushed garlic, the flavour becomes milder. The chemical reactions in the clove take up to a minute to occur, so wait before adding crushed garlic to the pan or a dressing to get the strongest flavour.

Peeling

Peeling garlic can be fiddly, but the larger and drier the cloves, the easier the job becomes. If you intend to crush the clove for cooking, the easiest way is to lay the blade of a large knife on top of the clove then press down on it with your hand. This breaks the skin away from the flesh quite easily.

Alternatively, you can buy a small rubber tube that peels the garlic cloves in seconds. Simply put the clove inside the tube, roll onto a work surface, and apply pressure to release the skin.

Crushing

Crushing or bashing garlic releases the maximum allicin and other sulphur-containing compounds from the clove, so results in the strongest flavours. There's a huge variety of garlic crushers available and most will do an adequate job, but a better-

Slicing

Peeled garlic can be easily sliced with a sharp knife. But if you are preparing a large quantity you may want to use a garlic slicer, which is like a mini mandolin. Sliced garlic has a slightly milder flavour than crushed garlic. It's great in stir-fries and curries and can be lightly fried to create a sweeter, nutty flavour. Take care not to burn the garlic when you fry it, though, as the flavour then becomes very bitter.

GARLIC FINGERS

When you're peeling, chopping and slicing cloves, garlic fingers become slightly unavoidable! However, there are a few antidotes you can try.

Some people soak their hands in lemon juice or vinegar, and then wash with warm water and soap, or you can try rubbing your hands against stainless steel, which is often conveniently close at hand in a kitchen. Apparently the molecules from the steel and the garlic bond and remove the smell from your fingers. (This also works for onions.) When you're peeling garlic, you often find some sneaks under your fingernails so I'd definitely recommend a nailbrush.

Green sprout

If your garlic is quite old and has already started to sprout, you may find a small green shoot on the inside of the clove when you cut it open. Although this is completely harmless and will not impair the flavour of the garlic, some people prefer to remove the shoot as it can be difficult to digest.

MEDICINAL MARVEL

Our ancestors intuited that garlic had enormous potential as a natural healer and these days scientific research is proving it all to be true. As well as vitamins and minerals, the cloves contain numerous health-giving sulphur compounds, of which allicin is the most potent. These are triggered into action when a garlic clove is chewed, crushed or cut, releasing its signature pungent aroma. They then set to work in harmony with the body to protect it against a variety of common ailments and more serious diseases. Millions of years of evolution have allowed the garlic bulb to perfect this self-protecting mechanism – all we have to do is consume it!

BUYING THE BEST

In order to enjoy the best flavour in your cooking, it's vital to use good-quality produce. It's great that garlic is so easy to come by these days and the local supermarket almost always has a good supply, though be aware that the kind of garlic on offer in supermarkets is generally not of the best quality.

Therefore, if you are looking for good-quality, long-lasting, flavoursome garlic, it is best to look a little further afield. Growing your own garlic from sound stock is a very good way to ensure an ample supply of fresh bulbs, but farmers' markets, farm shops and online are also good sources, and often offer a wide range of varieties.

Top tips for buying good garlic

♦ Always buy the bulbs intact and without cloves missing. Once the bulb is broken up, its life is shortened.

♦ Test the bulb for firmness – the firmer the cloves, the better. Any softness suggests the bulb is old and either won't last much longer or may already have started to go powdery on the inside.

♦ Avoid any garlic with green shoots. If small green shoots have started to appear at the tip of the cloves, the garlic has already started to sprout. You can still use the garlic, but it won't last as long as a fresher bulb.

HEALTH BURST

Allicin is the source of garlic's goodness and because it is partially destroyed by cooking, you'll get the greatest health boost if you use it raw or slightly cooked. Quite a few of the recipes that follow use garlic in this state and so preserve its optimum health-giving properties. However, don't be afraid that cooking garlic removes all the benefits as in fact it leads to other sulphur compounds being created which are also extremely beneficial to your health.

Storing

The best place to keep it is somewhere dry, to prevent mould, at room temperature, to inhibit sprouting, and somewhere with good air circulation. A pot with ventilation holes is ideal. Avoid plastic to prevent mould. Only store green garlic in the fridge and do not freeze green or dry garlic as the texture will change. Properly stored garlic can last for months.

STARTERS
& SOUPS

GARLIC & TOMATO TARTE TATIN *VEGETARIAN

This variation on the traditional tarte tatin melts in the mouth and makes an impressive dinner-party starter or summer lunch dish.

Serves 6

For the caramelised garlic
3–4 garlic bulbs, cloves peeled
Olive oil
1 tablespoon balsamic vinegar
2 teaspoons light brown sugar
Sprig each of rosemary and thyme, finely chopped
1 teaspoon salt

For the tomatoes
Olive oil
4 ripe plum tomatoes, cut lengthways (or a punnet of ripe cherry tomatoes, halved)
3 teaspoons light brown sugar
Salt and freshly ground black pepper

For the pastry
Ready-rolled puff pastry sheet, cut to fit over a 20cm oven-proof frying pan
1 egg, beaten

To garnish
250g feta cheese, crumbled
Sprigs of thyme

1. Preheat the oven to 200°C/fan 180°C/gas mark 6.

2. Put the garlic cloves in a small pan with water to cover and bring to the boil. Boil for 3 minutes then drain and dry the cloves and the pan. Return the garlic to the pan along with a glug of olive oil and fry for a further 3 minutes. Add 200ml water and the balsamic vinegar and boil for 10 minutes, or until most of the liquid has evaporated.

4. In the meantime, for the tomatoes pour a glug of olive oil onto a large plate and mix in the brown sugar and plenty of salt and pepper. Place the tomatoes, cut side down, into the oil ensuring each is well covered.

5. Heat a small glug of olive oil in the ovenproof frying pan and transfer the tomatoes, cut side down, into the pan. Fry for about 5 minutes, or until they start to go sticky, then remove from the heat.

6. By now most of the liquid should have evaporated from the garlic. Add the sugar, herbs and salt, and continue to fry until the cloves begin to brown. Remove from the heat then transfer the cloves to the frying pan and arrange around the tomatoes.

7. Place the pastry sheet over the tomatoes and garlic, tucking the edges of the pastry neatly into the pan. Brush with the beaten egg then place in the oven for 25 minutes, or until golden brown. Remove and cool slightly.

8. Take a large heatproof serving plate and place over the pan. Protecting your hands with oven mitts and holding the plate and pan firmly together, carefully flip the pan and the plate, then lift off the pan.

9. Sprinkle with the feta cheese and garnish with a thyme sprig or two. Serve with rocket or watercress.

CEVICHE   *DAIRY-FREE

A Latin American classic, ceviche is traditionally made with raw fish marinated in citrus juices and other flavourings, which depend on the regional variation. The acidity of the juice changes the chemical structure of the fish in a similar way to cooking, but leaves it with a wonderfully fresh texture and taste. For me, this dish is all about the incredible 'zing' on the palate and so I like to add plenty of chilli, garlic and cayenne.

Serves 4 as an appetiser

400g bream, sea bass,
   lemon sole fillets
   or other very fresh
   white fish, skinned
   and all bones removed
1 small red onion, very
   finely sliced
1 celery stick, very finely
   sliced
1–2 red chillis, deseeded
   and finely sliced
1 teaspoon cayenne pepper
2 garlic cloves
Juice of 3 limes
Juice of 1 lemon
A handful of coriander,
   roughly chopped
A handful of mint, roughly
   chopped
Sea salt

1. Make sure the fish fillets are completely bone and skin-free, then slice them across the grain into 1cm-thick pieces

2. Place the fish in a large bowl and add the onion, celery, chillis and cayenne. Crush in the garlic and pour over the citrus juices, carefully turning the ingredients with a wooden spoon to mix them thoroughly. Make sure the fish is completely covered in citrus juice.

3. Place the bowl in the fridge for at least 2 hours to allow the fish to 'cook' in the marinade. You will be able to tell when it's ready as the fish flesh will have become opaque.

4. Stir through the coriander and mint, sprinkle with salt and serve immediately on one large sharing plate or in small dishes with the juices from the bottom of the bowl poured over.

GARLIC
BLOODY MARY

The wicked combination of garlic, tomatoes and vodka makes for a punchy cocktail or hair-of-the-dog concoction. Perhaps not the healthiest way to consume your daily dose of garlic, but definitely a fun means of testing the wonder herb's reputation as a hangover cure. Alternatively, omit the vodka and drink your Garlic Virgin Mary guilt-free. Without vodka it's actually a brilliant way to top up on your raw garlic intake. Prepare ahead and refrigerate overnight to get the best flavours.

Makes 4 tall glasses

750ml tomato juice
Juice of 1 lemon
Juice of 1 lime
1 tablespoon freshly grated
 horseradish
1 tablespoon Worcestershire
 sauce
2 garlic cloves, crushed
1 teaspoon Tabasco
Salt and freshly ground
 black pepper to taste
Good-quality vodka
Celery sticks and ice cubes,
 to serve

1. Place all the ingredients, apart from the seasoning and vodka, in a blender and combine well. Season to taste then refrigerate until thoroughly chilled. The flavour improves the longer you leave it, so try to leave for at least 1 hour and overnight if possible. This virgin mixture will keep in the fridge for a week so.

2. Put a few ice cubes in each glass, pour in a measure (or two) of vodka then top with the Garlic Bloody Mary mixture. Alternatively, pour the virgin mixture without the alcohol, either straight or on the rocks. Serve with a stick of celery in each glass.

VIETNAMESE CHICKEN BROTH *DAIRY-FREE

Warming, invigorating, low fat and incredibly tasty, I love to eat this soup any day; although it's particularly good for anyone with a cold. You can adjust the chilli to taste.

Serves 4

750ml chicken stock
1 sachet instant miso soup
4 garlic cloves
A thumb-sized piece of ginger, cut into fine matchsticks
1–2 red chillis, deseeded and finely sliced
2 skinless chicken breasts
½ tablespoon sunflower oil
Sea salt and freshly ground black pepper
100g egg noodles
2 pak choi, chopped
1 tablespoon soy sauce
Juice of ½ lime
2 spring onions, sliced
A large handful of coriander

1. In a saucepan, heat the stock until simmering then remove from the heat and add the miso, stirring until dissolved. While the stock is still hot, finely chop two garlic cloves and add to the stock with all the ginger and chillis. Cover with a lid and leave to infuse.

2. Using a sharp knife, score the chicken breasts deeply three to four times across the top, then brush with sunflower oil and crush a garlic clove over each one, rubbing it into the meat. Fry for a few minutes on each side until browned but not completely cooked through.

3. Place the chicken on a chopping board and slice into strips. Add the chicken, noodles and chopped pak choi to the infused stock, return to the heat and simmer for a few minutes, until the noodles and chicken are cooked.

4. Add the soy sauce and lime juice and serve immediately in large bowls with a sprinkling of spring onion and coriander on top. Eat with chopsticks for the noodles and a spoon to scoop up the tasty broth.

IMMUNITY-BOOSTING SOUP
*VEGETARIAN *DAIRY-FREE

This clear broth does wonders if you're feeling congested and makes a very effective immune booster too. The large amount of garlic may surprise you, but trust me, the flavour is fantastic. Shiitake mushrooms are a symbol of longevity in Asia and an excellent source of selenium, a known antioxidant that plays a vital role in boosting the immune system.

Serves 4

30g dried shiitake, porcini and oyster mushrooms (add extra fresh shiitake mushrooms if available)
1 tablespoon olive oil
1 medium white onion, finely chopped
A thumb-sized piece of ginger, peeled and grated
1 whole garlic bulb, peeled
1 vegetable stock cube
Juice of 1 lemon
Sea salt and freshly ground black pepper

1. Pour boiling water (250ml) over the dried mushrooms in a bowl and leave them to soak for 10 minutes.

2. In the meantime, heat the oil in a heavy-based ovenproof pan. Add the onion and ginger then crush in all the garlic cloves. Fry gently until softened and aromatic.

3. Add the mushrooms and their water to the pan, plus any fresh mushrooms, then stir in the stock and the lemon juice.

4. Season then gently simmer with the lid on for at least 2 hours. Alternatively, transfer the pan to a low oven (about 120°C). Season to taste before serving with crusty bread.

GAZPACHO *VEGETARIAN *DAIRY-FREE

Hot summer lunches are an ideal time to serve this very flavoursome and refreshing, cold soup. It can be difficult to get raw garlic into your diet and this is an excellent option. If the weather is very hot, or if you haven't had time to chill the soup well, you can just add a few ice cubes before serving, as the Spaniards do.

Serves 6

1kg very ripe, good-quality tomatoes, roughly chopped
2 spring onions, chopped
3 garlic cloves
1 large cucumber, chopped
75ml olive oil
Juice of 1 lemon
2 tablespoons sherry vinegar
A handful of fresh basil leaves, finely chopped
A few stems of fresh flat-leaf parsley, finely chopped

For the garnish
2 slices of white bread, cubed
Olive oil, for frying
½ red pepper, finely diced
Cucumber, finely diced
Salt and pepper

1. Put the tomatoes, spring onions, garlic and most of the cucumber (retain a small amount for the garnish) into a blender and whizz until smooth. Pass through a fine sieve to remove most of the pulp.

2. Put the mixture back in the blender and slowly add the olive oil, lemon juice and sherry vinegar until combined before adding the basil and parsley. Be careful not to blend the herbs for too long as you want them to remain finely chopped, not puréed. Chill in the fridge.

3. To make the garnish, gently fry the bread in a little olive oil to make croûtons. To serve, season the gazpacho well before transferring to bowls and topping with the chopped vegetables and croûtons.

The secret to a great gazpacho is to use really ripe, good-quality tomatoes. Big, plump, fleshy ones are the best as they have fewer seeds, but anything sweet and delicious will help to produce a tasty soup.

BRUSCHETTA

This classic Italian antipasto is a delicious and simple way to include raw garlic in your diet. Any good-quality, fresh bread can be used, though I prefer ciabatta, and you can try adding different toppings, such as pesto, cheese, anchovies, cured meats or grilled vegetables.

Serves 4

1 small ciabatta loaf, cut into 2cm slices on the diagonal
Extra virgin olive oil
4 garlic cloves, peeled
6 very ripe vine tomatoes, diced
A small handful of fresh basil leaves, torn
Sea salt and freshly ground black pepper

1. Brush each side of the ciabatta slices with olive oil then toast under the grill on both sides.

2. While the bread is still hot, rub with the raw garlic cloves, top with the chopped tomatoes and basil leaves then drizzle with olive oil and season well.

GARLIC, ONION & THYME FRITTATA

*VEGETARIAN *GLUTEN FREE

This flavourful Italian omelette borrows potatoes from the Spanish tortilla, and is delicious as an antipasto or a simple Sunday-night supper dish. Serve with a fresh, crunchy salad, drizzled with classic vinaigrette (see page 78).

Serves 4 as a main or 6 as an antipasto

2 large potatoes, peeled and sliced to a pound-coin thickness
2 tablespoons olive oil
Knob of butter
4 small onions, or 2 large, thinly sliced
A large handful of fresh thyme sprigs, leaves only, plus extra sprigs to garnish
3 garlic cloves
6 eggs
Salt and freshly ground black pepper

1. Bring a pan of salted water to the boil and blanch the sliced potatoes for 3 minutes. Take care not to overcook them or they will fall apart in the frying pan. Drain in a colander to allow the steam to escape and set aside.

2. Heat the oil and butter in a non-stick frying pan then add the onions and fry over a low heat for 5 minutes, stirring occasionally. Add the thyme leaves, crush in the garlic with a pinch of salt and cook for a further 2 minutes.

3. Add the potatoes to the pan, carefully turning them to coat in the oil and butter. Add more oil if necessary. Cook for a further 5 minutes on a medium heat.

4. Meanwhile, beat the eggs with a good pinch of salt and some freshly ground black pepper then pour the egg mixture into the pan.

5. Cook on a low heat until the frittata starts to come away from the sides of the pan, then place the pan under the grill until the top of the frittata has browned slightly. The perfect frittata should be golden brown on the outside and slightly soft inside.

6. Serve the frittata directly from the pan or, if you're feeling confident, slide it out of the pan onto a plate and garnish with a couple of thyme sprigs.

AVOCADO GARLIC PRAWNS *GLUTEN-FREE

This combination is packed full of goodness and makes a very easy starter or lunch dish.

Serves 4

Knob of butter
500g raw fresh prawns, peeled, deveined
3 garlic cloves
1 tablespoon sweet chilli sauce
2 ripe avocados, peeled, halved, stones removed
Juice of 1 lemon
Salt and freshly ground black pepper
A bunch of fresh chives, finely chopped, to garnish

1. Heat the butter in a heavy-based frying pan or wok over a high heat. Throw in the prawns, quickly crush in the garlic then stir until the prawns are cooked through. Once cooked, stir through the sweet chilli sauce.

2. Place half an avocado on each plate and top with the cooked prawns. Squeeze plenty of lemon juice over the prawns, season with salt and freshly ground pepper then sprinkle with chopped chives.

COURGETTE FRITTERS *DAIRY-FREE

These are best made with very fresh courgettes as they give off less water. If your grated courgettes seem watery, sprinkle them with salt and leave for 15 minutes. Then place them in a clean tea towel and wring out some of the liquid into the sink.

Serves 4 as a starter

2 medium courgettes, grated
100g mozzarella, grated
A handful of fresh mint
   leaves, finely chopped
2 garlic cloves
Salt and freshly ground
   black pepper
4 tablespoons flour
2 tablespoons olive oil
Sweet chilli dipping sauce,
   to serve

1. Place the grated courgettes, mozzarella and chopped mint into a large bowl. Crush in the garlic cloves, season with salt and freshly ground black pepper, then mix everything together.

2. Add in the flour and 1 tablespoon of olive oil and stir well until the ingredients start to bind. If the mixture seems too wet, add more flour. Shape the mixture into golf-ball-sized pieces, then flatten.

3. Heat the remaining olive oil in a non-stick frying pan over a medium heat. Fry the fritters for 2–3 minutes on each side until golden brown.

4. Serve straight away with sweet chilli dipping sauce.

To maximise garlic's health-promoting potential, leave it for around 10 minutes after you have prepared it, to allow time for the alliin to be converted into allicin while the enzyme is still active.

GARLIC, CUMIN &
BEETROOT FRITTERS
*VEGETARIAN *DAIRY-FREE *GLUTEN-FREE

The brilliant colour of these sweet and delicious mouthfuls make a wonderful starter to serve alongside freshly made tzatziki dip (see page 80) for dunking. Increase the quantities and pile them high for impressive party nibbles.

Makes 12 small fritters

1 dessertspoon cumin seeds
4 large raw beetroots, peeled and grated
4 tablespoons flour, plus extra for shaping fritters
2 garlic cloves
Salt and freshly ground black pepper
3 tablespoons olive oil
Tzatziki (page 80), to serve

1. Heat a frying pan, add the cumin seeds and toast over a high heat for 2 minutes to release their flavour.

2. In a bowl, combine the grated beetroot, flour and cumin seeds then crush in the garlic cloves and sprinkle with salt and pepper.

3. Use your hands to bring all the ingredients together, squeezing the mixture to absorb all the flour.

4. With wet hands, shape the mixture into small balls. (This can be a little fiddly but don't worry; the beetroot will hold its shape once in the oil.) Sprinkle some flour onto a plate and coat the balls in the flour.

5. Heat the olive oil in a non-stick frying pan over a medium heat. Carefully place the beetroot balls into the pan, fry on each side until crispy then place on kitchen paper to absorb excess oil.

6. Serve straight away with tzatziki dip.

For a more formal dish, try serving these fritters on individual plates with tzatziki drizzled over the top. Accompany with a small watercress salad on the side. The flavours work perfectly and, not only that, it looks beautiful too.

SIDES
& SALADS

OAK-SMOKED GARLIC DAUPHINOISE

*VEGETARIAN *GLUTEN-FREE

I lived in Paris for a few years, sharing an apartment with a Canadian girl who was writing a French cookery book. I gave her smoked garlic from the farm and she went crazy, developing a smoked garlic dauphinoise for her book. Since it's hard to say whether or not smoked garlic has any health benefits, you can substitute it with ordinary garlic if you wish – it adds a great flavour too.

Serves 4–6

1kg waxy firm potatoes, thinly sliced
Sea salt and freshly ground black pepper
1 teaspoon nutmeg, freshly grated
1 bulb oak-smoked garlic, cloves (or 3–4 ordinary garlic cloves), peeled
500ml full-cream milk or milk mixed with cream
50g butter, cut into slivers

1. Preheat the oven to 190°C/fan 170°C/gas mark 5.

2. Place half the sliced potatoes in a large ovenproof gratin dish. Cover with a layer of seasoning then grate the garlic cloves over the top.

3. Tip the remainder of the potato slices into the dish, spreading them out evenly. Season again then pour over the milk, or milk and cream, and lay the butter slivers on the top.

4. Bake in the oven until all the liquid has been absorbed and the top has browned, about 1–1½ hours.

5. Serve with roasted meat and green vegetables.

This dish represents the ultimate comfort food. It's all about the long, slow cooking process so don't rush it. Check the dish halfway through and, if necessary, push the potatoes down so the cream is able to swim over and bubble on top. When it's ready it should be really brown and crispy so make sure it's finished off to perfection.

ROASTED GARLIC POTATOES *DAIRY-FREE

Good roast potatoes are to die for and once you taste this simple variation, well, you might have to die twice!

Serves 4–6

1kg new potatoes
4 tablespoons olive oil
Salt and freshly ground
　black pepper
1 large garlic bulb, separated
　into unpeeled cloves
1 lemon, halved
A few sprigs of rosemary,
　leaves only

1. Preheat the oven to 200°C/fan 180°C/gas mark 6.

2. Bring a large pan of salted water to the boil. Carefully add the potatoes and boil for around 7 minutes, or until they offer no resistance to a knife.

3. Drain the potatoes then cut them in half and return to the pan. Holding a lid on the pan, shake the potatoes around to fluff up the edges. Now toss with the olive oil, salt and freshly ground black pepper, juice of the lemon and rosemary leaves.

4. Spread the potatoes in a roasting tin and distribute the garlic cloves among them. Add the lemon halves to the tin then roast for 40 minutes, or until golden brown and crunchy. Discard the lemon halves before serving.

SPICY PURPLE
SPROUTING BROCCOLI

You can use this as a sauce served with noodles or as an accompaniment to grilled chicken.

Serves 4

600g purple sprouting
  broccoli or curly kale
1 heaped teaspoon sesame
  seeds
½ tablespoon olive oil
½ tablespoon sesame oil
5 garlic cloves, finely sliced
A thumb-sized piece of
  ginger, finely sliced
1 red chilli, deseeded and
  finely diced
1 tablespoon white wine
  vinegar
1 tablespoon light soy sauce

1. Bring a large pan of salted water to the boil. Add the broccoli and blanch for 3-4 minutes, then drain and set aside.

2. Meanwhile, heat a small frying pan, add the sesame seeds and toast over a medium heat until they start to pop, about 2 minutes. Set aside.

3. In another frying pan, heat the oils over a medium heat then add the garlic, ginger and chilli, and fry gently for 2 minutes.

4. Add the broccoli and turn to coat with the oil. Add the vinegar and soy sauce and cook for a further 2 minutes.

5. Serve with the sesame seeds sprinkled over.

For those wishing to reduce
their salt intake, garlic makes
a great alternative.
It adds substantial flavour to
your cooking and means
you'll need to use far less salt.

SOM TAM *DAIRY-FREE

Any visior to Thailand will have come across this fantastic, fresh, hot and spicy dish made from green (unripe) papayas. It's hard to replicate the exact flavours here but this combination comes quite close. Always use very unripe papaya, never the ripe orange kind.

Serves 4

1 large green papaya, peeled, deseeded (or 1 unripe mango, stone removed, or 1 firm cucumber, deseeded)
5 garlic cloves
3 red chillies, finely chopped
Large pinch of salt
1 teaspoon dried shrimp or shrimp paste
1 tablespoon fish sauce
Juice of 2 limes
1 tablespoon sugar
4 cherry tomatoes, cut into very small segments
3 heaped tablespoons beansprouts
4 tablespoons crushed peanuts

1. Shred the papaya (or mango or cucumber) into long, thin matchsticks.

2. Using a pestle and mortar, crush the garlic, chillies and salt. Add a small handful of the papaya and the dried shrimp or shrimp paste and gently pound until some of the juices are released.

3. Transfer to a bowl and stir in the rest of the ingredients, reserving some of the peanuts to sprinkle on top before serving.

The raw freshness of this dish not only gives a beautiful crunchy texture and delicious flavours but also makes it very nutritious. Surprisingly filling and very easy to prepare, it makes a great light lunch alternative to your average sandwich.

WARM LENTIL
& HALLOUMI SALAD

*VEGETARIAN *GLUTEN-FREE

My idea of heaven. Halloumi never fails to please in this quick and easy way to a delicious, healthy and filling lunch.

Serves 4

150g puy lentils
1 teaspoon Marigold Swiss
   Vegetable Bouillon Powder,
   or 1 gluten-free vegetable
   stock cube
½ red onion, finely sliced
1 green chilli, deseeded and
   finely sliced
2 tablespoons good-quality
   olive oil
2 garlic cloves
1 tablespoon olive oil
250g halloumi, sliced
2 small courgettes, cut into
   ribbons with a peeler
50g pomegranate seeds
A handful of chopped fresh
   coriander, including stalks
Sea salt and freshly ground
   black pepper

1. Cover the lentils with cold water and bring to the boil. Add the vegetable stock and cook for 15–20 minutes, or until the lentils are tender. Drain well.

2. While the lentils are still warm, place them in a large bowl. Add the onion, chilli and olive oil then crush in the garlic cloves and stir well.

3. For the halloumi, heat the oil in a frying pan over a medium heat. Add the halloumi and fry

on each side until golden. Stir the courgettes, pomegranate seeds and coriander into the bowl with the lentils. Season to taste.

4. Top the lentil mixture with the halloumi slices and serve.

You can add garlic to almost any salad, either in a salad dressing or as very thin, lightly fried garlic slices, scattered over as a topping. Take great care not to burn the garlic though as this will make it taste very bitter.

GARLIC & ROSEMARY FOCACCIA *VEGETARIAN *DAIRY-FREE

*Makes 1 large
or 2 medium-sized loaves*

400g plain strong white flour,
    plus extra for dusting
7g packet fast action yeast
1 teaspoon salt
400ml warm water
1–2 teaspoons honey or sugar
4 tablespoons olive oil, plus
    extra for oiling
4 garlic cloves
3 sprigs of fresh rosemary,
    leaves only, finely chopped
Sea salt

Including garlic in
bread dough itself,
I found out the hard
way, can impair the
dough's ability to rise.
This recipe avoids this
pitfall by adding the
garlic as a topping.

Focaccia is very easy to make and is always popular with the whole family. My children devour it.

1. Place the flour, yeast and 1 teaspoon of salt in a large bowl and make a well in the middle.

2. Fill a measuring jug with just over 300ml of warm water and stir in the honey or sugar and olive oil. Pour most of this mixture into the bowl of flour, stirring with a wooden spoon or your fingers to bring the dough together. Add a little more water if necessary until the dough has a soft, slightly wet consistency that is easily workable.

3. Place the dough on a lightly floured work surface then knead for at least 10 minutes, until it becomes elastic and smooth.

4. Clean, dry and oil the bowl before placing the dough back in, then cover with oiled clingfilm. Leave to rise in a warm place until it has doubled in size.

5. Preheat the oven to 200°C/fan 180°C/gas mark 6.

6. Once the dough has risen, knock it back on a clean floured work surface. Shape the dough into one or two oval-shaped flattish loaves, transfer onto baking trays then leave to rise again for about 20 minutes.

7. In the meantime, pour 2 tablespoons of olive oil into a small bowl, crush in the garlic cloves, tip in the chopped rosemary and stir well.

8. When the dough has risen, make holes in it with your fingertips then pour over the garlic and rosemary mixture, making sure it gets into the holes.

9. Sprinkle with plenty of sea salt and place in the oven to bake for 30 minutes, or until golden and hollow-sounding when tapped on the bottom. Turn out onto a wire rack to cool.

THE BEST CHEESY GARLIC BREAD *VEGETARIAN

Garlic and bread can be combined in a huge variety of ways. We've tried many at the farm and can guarantee this one will vanish off the table more quickly than a vampire on a sunny day.

Makes 1 baguette

100g butter
3–4 large garlic cloves
100g mozzarella
100g Cheddar
A handful of fresh herbs – parsley, basil, marjoram and oregano all work well
1 fresh baguette, sliced diagonally at 4–5cm intervals
Paprika for sprinkling

1. Preheat the oven to 200°C/fan 180°C/gas mark 6.

2. Put all the filling ingredients in a blender or food processor and blend until fully incorporated.

3. Generously spread the filling between the baguette slices. Wrap the baguette loosely in foil then place in the oven for 20–25 minutes, until the filling has melted.

4. Remove from the oven, open the foil and sprinkle with paprika. Leaving the foil open, return the baguette to the oven for a few minutes, until the crust is golden brown.

TOASTED CIABATTA

*DAIRY-FREE

At our café, the brilliant chef likes to use the different varieties of garlic we grow to suit different dishes. He recommends strong-flavoured Chesnok Wight for this garlic bread.

Makes 2 loaves

125g salted butter, softened
3 fat Chesnok Wight cloves,
   or other strong-flavoured
   garlic variety, finely
   chopped
1 sprig of fresh rosemary,
   leaves only, finely chopped
2 ciabatta loaves, cut
   lengthways
Chilli flakes (optional)

1. Mix the butter with the garlic and rosemary.

2. Spread the ciabatta with a thick layer of garlic butter. Place on a grill tray and grill until golden brown.

3. Cut the toasted ciabatta on a diagonal and serve. Add a light sprinkling of chilli flakes to spice it up if you wish.

MAINS

CHICKEN WITH
40 GARLIC CLOVES

*DAIRY-FREE *GLUTEN-FREE

Happily, some 1970s dinner-party classics are making a comeback, including this traditional French dish, which makes the most of garlic's sweet, rich flavour by cooking the cloves encased in their skins. Once cooked, the cloves can be served as they are, so that guests can squeeze garlic onto their plates. Alternatively, use the extracted flesh to create a deliciously creamy sauce.

Serves 4–6

2 celery stalks, chopped
1 large organic chicken
   (about 1.6kg)
2 large sprigs of rosemary
2 large sprigs of thyme
3–4 large garlic bulbs
2 tablespoons olive oil
Salt and freshly ground
   black pepper
2 bay leaves
1 large carrot, diced
1 small onion, cut into
   wedges
2 large glasses of Marsala

1. Preheat the oven to 200°C/fan 180°C/gas mark 6.

2. Place the chopped celery, 1 sprig of each herb and a handful of unpeeled garlic cloves into the chicken cavity.

3. Place half the remaining cloves in a lidded casserole, put the chicken on top, brush with olive oil and season well. Arrange the bay leaves, carrot, onion and remaining herbs and garlic cloves around the chicken.

4. Drizzle with olive oil then pour over the Marsala. Cover and roast for at least 1 hour 20 minutes, or until the chicken is tender and the juices run clear when the flesh is pierced with a skewer.

5. Either serve with toasted bread, spread with the soft flesh of the garlic cloves, or whisk the garlic flesh with the juices from the bottom of the casserole to make a creamy sauce.

SLOW LAMB WITH YOGURT MINT SAUCE

Don't be put off by the long cooking time of this dish. It's incredibly quick and easy to prepare, and slow cooking allows the meat to become beautifully tender as well as giving fantastic depth of flavour. You can leave it to cook overnight or prepare it in the morning for supper.

Serves 4–6

2kg shoulder of lamb
Salt and freshly ground
   black pepper
2 tablespoons olive oil
3 onions, sliced
4 carrots, quartered
   lengthways
1 garlic bulb or 8–10 cloves,
   peeled but left whole
1 bay leaf
250ml white wine
250ml vegetable, beef or
   chicken stock

For the sauce
3 tablespoons Greek yogurt
2 sprigs of fresh mint,
   leaves only
Sea salt and freshly
   ground black pepper

1. Preheat the oven to 120°C/fan 100°C/gas mark ½.

2. Season the lamb well with salt and freshly ground black pepper.

3. Heat the olive oil in a large, flame-proof lidded casserole over a high heat. Add the lamb joint to the casserole and fry for about 15 minutes, turning regularly, until browned all over. Turn down the heat.

4. Add the vegetables, garlic cloves and bay leaf around the meat, then pour in the wine and stock. Bring to the boil before placing the casserole in the oven. Cook for up to 7 hours. (Although the meat will be cooked after about 5 hours, it's best left for the full time if possible.) Turn the meat halfway through cooking.

5. Remove the casserole from the oven and transfer the lamb and vegetables to a serving dish. Cover with foil and return to the oven to keep warm.

6. To make the sauce, skim off any excess fat from the casserole then place the dish over a medium heat. Boil until the liquid has reduced by about a quarter, then add the yogurt and mint leaves, stirring well. Return to a simmer, remove the mint leaves and add seasoning if needed.

7. Pour the sauce into a jug and serve the lamb with mash and a steamed green vegetable, such as spring greens.

MUSHROOM PIZZA

Homemade pizza is as satisfying to prepare as it is to eat. This recipe is a re-creation of a mouth-watering pizza I was served in Verona. It has no tomato sauce, which means it's even quicker to make – and you'll be surprised that you don't even miss it. Serve with a rocket salad.

Makes 2 large pizzas

For the base
500g plain flour, plus extra
    for dusting
1 sachet (6g) fast-action
    dried yeast
2 tablespoons olive oil
2 teaspoons sugar or honey

For the topping
300g porcini or other
    flavoursome mushrooms,
    sliced
A few sprigs of fresh
    rosemary, finely chopped
4 garlic cloves, peeled
Olive oil
Salt and freshly ground
    black pepper
100g buffalo mozzarella,
    chopped
4 tablespoons grated
    Parmesan

1. To make the base, mix the flour and yeast in a large bowl and make a well in the centre. In a jug, mix the olive oil and sugar or honey with 300ml warm water, then pour into the well of the flour mixture and gradually mix to form a soft and slightly sticky dough.

2. Transfer the dough to a lightly floured work surface and lightly flour your hands. Knead the dough by hand for at least 10 minutes, until smooth and pliable. Place the dough back in the bowl and cover with oiled clingfilm. Leave to rise for 45 minutes or until doubled in size.

3. Preheat the oven to 250°C/fan 230°C/gas mark 10.

4. Place the mushrooms and chopped rosemary sprigs into a bowl. Crush in the garlic, pour over a good glug of olive oil, season with salt and freshly ground pepper and combine well.

5. Remove the clingfilm from the dough and divide it into two balls. On a lightly floured work surface, carefully stretch them out into round bases about 5mm thick.

6. Cover each base with the mushroom mixture then top with mozzarella and Parmesan.

7. Bake the pizzas in the oven until the bases are crisp and golden-brown around the edges and the cheese has melted.

ROASTED BUTTERNUT SQUASH RISOTTO *VEGETARIAN

As well as being sweet and delicious, butternut squash is packed with vitamins and minerals, adding an extra health kick to this tasty vegetarian supper.

Serves 4

1 large butternut squash,
cut into large chunks,
seeds removed
3–4 large garlic cloves, peeled
1 tablespoon olive oil, plus
extra for drizzling
A few sprigs of thyme, plus
1 tablespoon chopped thyme
Salt and freshly ground
black pepper
50g butter
1 large onion, finely chopped
250g Arborio risotto rice
125ml white wine
1 litre good-quality vegetable
stock
A handful of freshly grated
vegetarian Parmesan, plus
extra to serve
A handful of toasted
pine nuts, to serve

1. Preheat the oven to 200°C/fan 180°C/gas mark 6.

2. Place the butternut squash in a large bowl. Crush in one or two garlic cloves, drizzle with olive oil, add the thyme sprigs and season well. Mix thoroughly, ensuring the squash gets a good oiling and the garlic is well distributed. Put the mixture in a large roasting tray and roast for 30–40 minutes, or until the edges of the squash begin to brown.

4. Remove the squash from the oven and allow it to cool slightly before scraping the flesh away from the skin into a bowl, removing any thyme twigs. Scrape any sticky juices into the bowl and mash the squash. Keep warm while making the risotto.

5. Heat the olive oil and a large knob of butter in a heavy-based pan, add the onion and gently fry until softened, about 2 minutes. Crush in 2 garlic cloves and gently fry for a further 2 minutes.

6. Add the rice and stir well so the grains become coated in the butter and oil. Pour in the wine and stir well until absorbed.

7. Add a ladleful of hot stock and stir until absorbed. Keep the pan simmering while gradually adding more stock and continuing to stir, until the rice is cooked al dente, about 15–20 minutes. The risotto should have a smooth and creamy consistency. Add more stock if necessary.

8. Remove from the heat and add the mashed squash, a large knob of butter, grated Parmesan, 1 tablespoon chopped thyme and seasoning to taste. Stir well.

9. Serve with toasted pine nuts and a sprinkling of grated or shaved Parmesan.

SPAGHETTI CARBONARA

Pasta sauces lend themselves particularly well to the addition of garlic. There are several ways of preparing this Italian favourite, but my recipe includes a good amount of garlic for enhanced flavour and health benefits.

Serves 4

1 tablespoon olive oil
6 thick slices of pancetta
   or streaky bacon, chopped
   into small pieces
4 shallots, finely diced
4 fat garlic cloves, finely
   chopped
4 large eggs
40g Parmesan, freshly grated
Freshly ground black pepper
500g good-quality fresh
   spaghetti
2 spring onions, chopped
A handful of fresh basil leaves,
   chopped
A handful of fresh parsley
   leaves, chopped

1. Heat the oil in a large frying pan over a medium heat and gently fry the pancetta, shallots and garlic for 5–7 minutes, or until the shallots have softened.

2. In a bowl, lightly beat the eggs and most of the grated Parmesan, reserving a little for the garnish. Season with a good amount of freshly ground black pepper.

3. Boil the pasta in a large pan of salted boiling water according to packet instructions, about 2–3 minutes.

4. Drain the cooked spaghetti then return to the pan, off the heat. Quickly add the pancetta, shallots and garlic and pour in the egg mixture, stirring well.

5. Add the spring onions, basil and parsley and stir well again.

6. Serve immediately, sprinkled with freshly ground black pepper and extra Parmesan.

When sautéing garlic, take great care to make sure it never turns more than pale gold to light brown in colour and never allow it to turn dark brown as this will impair the flavour. If you wish to keep the garlic flavours subtle, it is best to lightly sauté the garlic very briefly in oil then, before it can turn brown, allow it to simmer with the juices of the other ingredients.

ASIAN FISH PARCEL

A magical trio of flavours – chilli, garlic and ginger – works particularly well in this quick and simple fish supper, which can be made using fresh or frozen fish.

Serves 4

Olive oil
4 large fillets of pollack, or
  other sustainable white,
  flaky fish
A thumb-sized piece of
  ginger, peeled and grated
8 garlic cloves, sliced
2 red chillis, finely sliced
4 tablespoons light soy sauce
½ tablespoon toasted
  sesame oil
2 pak choi, finely sliced
2 spring onions, finely
  chopped, to garnish
A handful of fresh coriander,
  roughly chopped,
  to garnish
200g steamed jasmine
  rice, to serve

1. Preheat the oven to 190°C/fan 170°C/gas mark 5.

2. Take four sheets of foil, large enough to loosely encase each fillet, and lay on a work surface. Brush one side of each sheet with olive oil.

3. Place a fish fillet in the centre of each sheet then arrange on a baking tray, bringing the sides of the sheets up around the fish.

4. Top each fillet with the ginger, garlic, chilli and soy sauce, then fold over the foil to seal. Transfer the tray to the oven and bake the parcels for 15–20 minutes. In the meantime, lightly sauté the pak choi in sesame oil for 3–4 minutes on a medium heat.

5. Serve the fish on a bed of jasmine rice alongside the pak choi with the juices from the parcels and garnished with chopped coriander and spring onions.

SPICY BEEF
& SCAPES STIR-FRY
*DAIRY-FREE

Garlic scapes bring a fantastic crunchy texture with fresh garlic flavours to all sorts of dishes.

Serves 4

2 tablespoons light soy sauce
A thumb-sized piece of
   ginger, peeled and grated
1 small red chilli
1 teaspoon sesame oil
2 large garlic cloves
500g sirloin steak, cut into
   thin strips
300g garlic scapes (or
   spring onions or garlic
   chives), cut into
   6cm lengths
2 tablespoons sunflower oil
1 red pepper, sliced
50ml hot beef stock
200g steamed white rice,
   to serve

1. Combine the soy sauce, ginger, chilli and sesame oil in a bowl. Crush in the garlic and add the steak, tossing to coat it completely. Let it stand for 15 minutes.

2. Blanche the scapes for 2 minutes in salted boiling water, drain and set aside.

3. Heat the oil in a wok and, on a high heat, fry the steak strips in 2 batches for about 2 minutes each. The meat should be browned on the outside but still pink in the middle. Heat the rest of the oil in the wok, add the red pepper and fry for a minute or so, then add the scapes, all the steak, any remaining juices from the marinade and the stock and stir-fry until piping hot. Serve immediately on plain rice.

The scape is the generic name for a flower stalk that emerges from the top of the plant, sometimes twisting and curling before growing straight up.

TANDOORI CHICKEN

This delicious Indian dish wouldn't be the same without garlic adding heat to the spicy yogurt marinade.

Serves 4

8 free-range organic
   chicken thighs, drumsticks
   or 4 breasts, skinned
Pinch of salt
Juice of 1 lemon
A thumb-sized piece of
   ginger, peeled and grated
6 garlic cloves, crushed
2 green chillies, finely
   chopped
2 teaspoons garam masala
2 teaspoons sumac
4 tablespoons Greek yogurt
30g butter

To serve
Juice of 1 lemon
1 red onion, finely sliced
Salt and freshly ground
   black pepper
2 handfuls of fresh mint
   leaves
4 tablespoons Greek yogurt
Flatbread

1. Cut a few incisions into the chicken pieces using a small, sharp knife. Place the chicken into a bowl then sprinkle over the salt, lemon juice and all the spices, massaging into the chicken until well coated.

2 Add the yogurt and mix with the chicken and spices. Cover and refrigerate overnight or for a minimum of 4 hours.

3. Preheat the oven to its highest setting.

4. Remove the chicken pieces from the yogurt and lay them in a roasting tin or on a baking tray, making sure they have plenty of room. Roast in the centre of the oven for 20 minutes. Halfway through cooking, add a knob of butter on top of the chicken to give it a nice browned finish.

5. Remove the chicken from the oven and leave to rest for 5 minutes.

6. To serve, squeeze the lemon juice over the onion slices and season. Pile the dressed onion and mint leaves onto a plate with the tandoori chicken and accompany with yogurt and flatbread on the side.

SPICY CHICKPEA & BROCCOLI CURRY

*GLUTEN-FREE *DAIRY-FREE

Not all curries include lots of garlic but many certainly benefit from its great base flavours. Frying crushed garlic and ginger together is one of my favourite ways to start a curry. This one is tasty, healthy and economical, and even more delicious the day after it's made.

Serves 4

2 tablespoons olive oil
1 onion, finely chopped
6 garlic cloves, crushed
A thumb-sized piece of
  ginger, grated
2 red chillies, deseeded and
  finely chopped
1 teaspoon turmeric
1 teaspoon ground cumin
2 teaspoons ground coriander
1 teaspoon garam masala
2 × 400g cans chickpeas
1 × 400g can chopped tomatoes
50g red lentils
6 tablespoons coconut cream
1 head of broccoli, chopped
  into small florets
Sea salt and freshly ground
  black pepper

To serve
2 handfuls of fresh
  coriander, chopped
200g brown rice, cooked

1. Heat the olive oil in a deep saucepan or a wok and fry the onion, garlic, ginger and chillies on a medium heat for 2 minutes.

2. Add the spices and fry for a further 5 minutes, adding more oil if necessary.

3. Pour in the chickpeas and tomatoes, add the lentils and coconut cream then simmer until the lentils have softened.

4. Add the broccoli and simmer for a further 5 minutes then season to taste.

5. Garnish with a sprinkling of coriander and serve with the brown rice.

Pairing ginger and garlic is one of the building blocks of Indian cuisine and ginger-garlic paste is an indispensable ingredient in many condiments and curries. You make it with equal quantities of garlic and ginger, blended together, and Indian cooks often make up huge batches as it's something they can guarantee they'll be using every day.

DIPS, SAUCES & DRESSINGS

AÏOLI

This extremely versatile garlic mayonnaise is originally from the Provence region in the south of France, which helps explain the origin of the name. 'Aï' is the Provençal word for garlic and 'oli' is from the Latin oleum, meaning oil. It works equally well served as a dip with steamed vegetables or as a sauce to accompany fish or meat.

Makes about 350ml

3 large garlic cloves, peeled
2 egg yolks
1 tablespoon Dijon mustard
300ml olive oil
Juice of ¼ lemon
Salt and freshly ground
    black pepper

1. Using a pestle and mortar, crush the garlic with a pinch of salt to form a paste.

2. In a bowl, whisk the garlic, egg yolks and mustard until well combined.

3. Add the olive oil in a steady stream and whisk until all the oil is absorbed and the mixture has thickened.

4. Add a squeeze of lemon juice and season to taste. If you'd like to use the aïoli as a sauce, whisk in a few drops of warm water to make it runnier.

CLASSIC HUMMUS

*VEGETARIAN *DAIRY-FREE *GLUTEN-FREE

We serve this hummus in The Garlic Farm café and the bowl is always returned as if it's been licked clean. Need I say more?

Serves 4

400g can chickpeas, drained
Juice of ½ lemon
1 heaped teaspoon cumin
3 garlic cloves, crushed
1 tablespoon chopped
   coriander
1 dessertspoon tahini
Large glug of mild olive oil
Large pinch of salt and
   cracked black pepper

1. Place all the ingredients in a food processor and whizz. To keep a good rustic chunkiness, don't blend for too long.

2. Serve with any combination of crudités or breadsticks or warmed pitta bread.

VINAIGRETTE

*VEGETARIAN *GLUTEN-FREE
*DAIRY-FREE

The use of sunflower oil instead of olive oil makes this dressing much lighter, making it the perfect partner for a crunchy green salad. Freshly made vinaigrette will keep in a jar for up to a week, or in a sealed container in the fridge for several weeks.

Makes about 100ml

2 tablespoons white wine
  vinegar
60ml sunflower oil
1 teaspoon Dijon mustard
1 garlic clove, crushed
Sea salt and freshly ground
  black pepper

1. Put the vinegar, oil, mustard and garlic in a screw-top jar and season. Cover the jar and shake well to combine.

2. Store in a cool place until ready to use, adding fresh herbs just before serving if desired.

GARLIC & CORIANDER YOGURT DRESSING

*VEGETARIAN *GLUTEN-FREE

This dressing will keep in a sealed container in the fridge for about 3 days.

Makes about 100ml

4 heaped tablespoons
  Greek-style yogurt
Juice of ¼ lemon
A 3cm-sized piece of ginger,
  peeled and grated
1 garlic clove, crushed
Small handful of fresh
  coriander, roughly
  chopped

1. Mix all the ingredients in a bowl until well combined.

TZATZIKI *VEGETARIAN *GLUTEN-FREE

One of my all-time favourites. Some recipes suggest salting the cucumber to remove excess moisture, but personally I don't think this is necessary if you use very fresh, crisp cucumbers and serve the dip straight away. In my experience, there are never any leftovers!

Makes about 400ml

½ large cucumber
2 garlic cloves
200ml thick Greek yogurt
100ml crème fraîche
1 tablespoon each finely
   chopped parsley and mint
1 tablespoon olive oil
Juice of ¼ lemon
Salt and freshly ground
   black pepper

1. Peel, deseed and finely dice the cucumber and crush the garlic. Simply stir all the ingredients together, adjusting the seasoning if necessary, then spoon into a serving bowl and garnish with a sprinkle of chopped mint.

2. Serve as an appetiser or snack with crudités (batons of raw carrot, celery, etc.), toasted pitta bread or crisps. Alternatively, tzatziki makes a refreshing side to sizzling lamb chops.

MOROCCAN DRESSING *VEGETARIAN *GLUTEN-FREE *DAIRY-FREE

This dressing will keep in a sealed container in the fridge for a week (photo on page 79).

Makes about 150ml

6 tablespoons extra virgin
   olive oil
3 tablespoons red wine
   vinegar
1 teaspoon sweet paprika
½ teaspoon ground cumin
1 garlic clove, finely chopped
Small handful of fresh flat-leaf
   parsley, finely chopped

1. Mix all the ingredients in a bowl until well combined.

PICKLED GARLIC, LEMON & LIMES

*VEGETARIAN *GLUTEN-FREE

Delicious homemade pickle has long been a favourite in our family, which is why we make and sell a huge range of pickles and chutneys at The Garlic Farm. And as we're constantly coming up with new creations, our range is growing by the year. This recipe is a real winner. I've chosen to share it in this book because it's very easy to make at home, unlike some of our recipes, which require a long list of ingredients and much more preparation time.

Makes 1 jar

3 tablespoons mustard seeds
1 tablespoon fenugreek seeds
2 tablespoons groundnut oil, for frying
1 teaspoon turmeric
1 tablespoon red chilli powder
3 unwaxed lemons, cut into small chunks
3 unwaxed limes, cut into small chunks (rinds on, seeds discarded)
2 garlic bulbs, cloves peeled
3 tablespoons sea salt

1. Using a pestle and mortar, bash the mustard and fenugreek seeds until they are slightly crushed.

2. Heat the oil in a pan and gently fry all the spices for 2 minutes, then add the fruit, garlic cloves and salt, stir and remove from the heat.

3. Place the mixture in an airtight container or jar. Try to choose a container that doesn't leave too much air when filled with the mixture.

4. Leave to mature in the fridge for at least 10 days, turning occasionally.

CUCUMBER KIMCHI

The Koreans have been eating this incredibly healthy dish with almost every meal for centuries, the earliest references to Kimchi being from at least 2600 years ago. It is made by part-fermenting vegetables, usually napa cabbage, with a combination of flavours and spices, including garlic. Here is a cucumber-based version which is relatively easy to prepare and the crispy crunch of the cucumber combined with garlic and chilli taste delicious.

Makes 1 large batch, enough for 2 large jars

700g small cucumbers (pickling cucumbers work best but large cucumbers also work)
2 tablespoons sea salt
½ onion, finely chopped
4 spring onions, sliced lengthways then chopped on the diagonal
4 garlic cloves
1 small red chilli, deseeded and finely chopped (optional)
1–2 tablespoons Korean chilli pepper powder, gochugaru (or any red chilli powder)
2 teaspoons honey
2 teaspoons vinegar

1. Wash and chop the cucumbers into smallish (3cm) pieces.

2. Place them in a large ceramic bowl and sprinkle with the salt, then leave at room temperature overnight or at least for a few hours.

3. Add the onion and spring onions to the cucumber, crush in the garlic cloves and then add the chilli, chilli powder, honey and vinegar. Mix all the ingredients together well.

4. Place the mixture in the fridge to cool. When cooled, you can eat this right away or, alternatively, transfer into two large sterilised jars, sharing out the juices from the bottom of the bowl and leave it to ferment at room temperature for a couple of days before putting it in the fridge. As the cucumbers will eventually lose their crunch, it is best to eat this kimchi within a week or so.

The beauty of this side dish or *banchan*, as the Koreans call it, is that it not only livens up your palate but is also the key to maintaining a healthy digestive system thanks to the presence of gut-friendly bacteria, *lactobacilli*. Western diets typically lack fermented foods and many would argue that this is of great detriment to our health.

HOT TOMATO SALSA *DAIRY-FREE

One of our best-selling relishes is a very hot tomato and garlic salsa called Vampire Relish. This is a variation that uses fresh tomatoes and will definitely ensure no fanged friends dare come to your party.

Serves 12–16

4 large vine-ripened
   tomatoes, roughly chopped
½ red onion, roughly chopped
2 garlic cloves, chopped
Juice of 1 lime
2 teaspoons dried chilli flakes
2 teaspoons chilli sauce
   (e.g. Tabasco), or to taste
1 tablespoon red wine vinegar
Salt and freshly ground
   black pepper to taste
A few sprigs of fresh parsley,
   finely chopped

1. Place all the ingredients, except the parsley, in a food processor. Blend carefully to keep the mixture slightly chunky.

2. Stir in the parsley, season to taste and refrigerate until needed. It tastes better if left for a couple of hours before serving with tortilla chips.

This classic pesto recipe and variation offer a simple yet delicious way of introducing more garlic into your diet – I'm always generous with the garlic, so you may vary the quantities to suit your taste. The sauce can be stirred into freshly cooked pasta, added to sandwiches or bruschetta, mixed into bean salads, spread over roasted meats or used as stuffing for chicken breasts.

CLASSIC PESTO *GLUTEN-FREE

30g pine nuts
A large bunch of fresh basil
   leaves
2 large garlic cloves, peeled
6 tablespoons olive oil
Juice of ¼ lemon
30g Parmesan, grated
Sea salt

1. Lightly toast the pine nuts in a frying pan, until they are pale golden brown.

2. Put the toasted pine nuts and remaining ingredients, except the Parmesan, in a food processor and pulse until the desired consistency is reached – I prefer pesto to have a little texture.

3. Stir in the grated Parmesan and add salt to taste.

GREEN GARLIC PESTO *GLUTEN-FREE

3 large green garlic bulbs,
   roots removed
2 garlic cloves, chopped
4 tablespoons olive oil
1 teaspoon salt
4 tablespoons mixed seeds
   (pine nuts, pumpkin seeds
   and sunflower seeds)
A good handful of fresh
   basil leaves
150g Parmesan or pecorino,
   finely grated
Sea salt

1. Finely chop the bulbs, stems and leaves.

2. Place all the ingredients, except the cheese, in a food processor and pulse until you reach the desired consistency.

3. Stir in the cheese and add salt to taste. Mix in more olive oil if the pesto is too dry.

THE BEST WHOLE
ROASTED GARLIC

*VEGETARIAN *DAIRY-FREE *GLUTEN-FREE

We've tried and tested so many different ways of roasting garlic at home and in our farm café. After much deliberation, this is our recommended method for the most succulent, squeezable, sweet cloves. You can serve the whole bulb alongside roasted meats.

Makes 1 per person

1 whole garlic bulb
  per person
Olive oil

1. Preheat the oven to 180°C/fan 160°C/gas mark 4.

2. Cover the outside of the bulb/s in olive oil. Loosely encase them in foil (you can use a roasting pot if you have one) then roast in the oven for 1 hour.

3. Unwrap the foil or remove the lid of the roasting pot and roast uncovered for a further 10 minutes.

4. To serve, slice the bulb horizontally; making a kind of lid that can be lifted up to spoon out the soft flesh of the cloves.

INDEX

WITH THANKS

To all my tasters and testers of everything from the sweet and delicious to the extremely experimental.

Special thanks to my husband Barnes for his unfailing support and my children Arlo and Freya for already being able to recognise a good garlic bulb.

To my dear friend and excellent cook, Columbine Mulvey for all her expert help, culinary tips, ideas and inspiration.

To my parents, without whom this book would not have been possible, for so many reasons other than the obvious. Thank you both.

To Kyle, Judith and Vicki at Kyle Books for all their hard work and their faith in this book.

To everyone at The Garlic Farm. Keep up the good work!

This condensed edition published in
Great Britain in 2016 by
Kyle Books, an imprint of Kyle Cathie Ltd
192–198 Vauxhall Bridge Road
London SW1V 1DX
general.enquiries@kylebooks.com
www.kylebooks.co.uk

First published in Great Britain in 2012
under the title *Garlic: The Mighty Bulb*

10 9 8 7 6 5 4 3 2 1

ISBN 978 0 85783 382 2

Project Editor: Claire Rogers
Designer: Helen Bratby
Photographer: Peter Cassidy
Illustrator: Jenni Desmond
Food and Props Stylist: Annie Rigg
Production: Nic Jones and Gemma John

A Cataloguing in Publication record
for this title is available from the British
Library.

Colour reproduction by ALTA London
Printed and bound in China by C&C Offset
Printing Co., Ltd.

Note: all eggs are free-range